Qabbalistic Teachings
and the
Tree of Life

By Manly P. Hall

ISBN: 978-1-63118-482-6

Esoteric Classics:
Studies in Kabbalah

Other Books in this Series and Related Titles

The Sepher Yetzirah and the Qabalah by M P Hall (978-1-63118-481-9)

The Kabbalah of Masonry & Related Writings by E Levi &c (978-1-63118-453-6)

History, Analysis and Secret Tradition of the Tarot by Hall &c (978-1-63118-445-1)

The Ceremony of Initiation: Analysis & Commentary (978-1-63118-473-4)

Crystal Vision Through Crystal Gazing by Achad (978-1-63118-455-0)

Magical Essays and Instructions by Florence Farr (978-1-63118-418-5)

Ancient Mysteries and Secret Societies by M P Hall (978-1-63118-410-9)

The Secrets of Enoch by Enoch (978-1-63118-449-9)

The Path of Light: A Manual of Maha-Yana Buddhism (978-1-63118-471-0)

The Rosicrucian Chemical Marriage by Christian Rosenkreuz (978-1-63118-458-1)

Ghosts in Solid Form by Gambier Bolton (978-1-63118-469-7)

American Indian Freemasonry by A C Parker (978-1-63118-460-4)

The Mysteries of Freemasonry & the Druids by M P Hall &c (978-1-63118-444-4)

Psalms of Solomon by King Solomon (978-1-63118-439-0)

The Leadbeater Reader: A Selection of Occult Essays (978-1-63118-483-3)

The Machinery of the Mind by Dion Fortune (978-1-63118-451-2)

The Gospel of the Nativity of Mary by St. Matthew (978-1-63118-448-2)

Buddhist Psalms by Shinran (978-1-63118-465-9)

Freemasonry and the Egyptian Mysteries by C W Leadbeater (978-1-63118-456-7)

Alchemy in the Nineteenth Century by H P Blavatsky (978-1-63118-446-8)

The Human Aura: Astral Colors and Thought Forms (978-1-63118-419-2)

Audio versions are also available on Audible, Amazon and Apple

Table of Contents

INTRODUCTION

The word "esoteric" can be difficult to define. Esotericism in general can be seen less as a system of beliefs and more as a category, which encompasses numerous, different systems of beliefs. It's a bit of juxtaposition, since the word "esoteric" indicates something that few people know about, while the term itself broadly covers numerous philosophies, practices, areas of study and belief systems.

In a greater sense, Esotericism acts as a storehouse for secret knowledge, which is often considered ancient (by *tradition, if not by fact)*, passed down from generation to generation, in private. At various times in history, simply possessing the knowledge of some of these subjects, was considered illegal and a jailable offence, if discovered. This usually included such general topics as Alchemy, Qabalah, Hermeticism, Occultism, Ceremonial Magic, Astrology, Divination, Rosicrucianism and so on. Collectively, these areas of study were often referred to as the esoteric sciences.

Sometimes, the outer garment of a subject isn't esoteric, while what is hidden beneath it, is. As an example, Freemasonry isn't necessarily esoteric by nature (at *least not anymore)*, but certain signs, passwords and handshakes given to the candidate during their initiation, are in fact, esoteric, in the sense that they are hidden from the general public.

Today, in the twenty-first century, such topics are readily available at bookstores across the country, and numerous mainsteam publishers offer beginners guides and coffee-table volumes on many of these subjects, intended for mass appeal. Books like *"The Secret"* have turned previously arcane topics into household knowledge. All that being the case, however, it isn't to say that there still aren't buried secrets to uncover, ancient wisdom being ignored and forgotten mysteries to be explored. In fact, it is often that we are only able to further our own studies by standing on the shoulders of these disappearing giants.

Lamp of Trismegistus is doing its part to help preserve humanity's esoteric history by making some of these classics available to those students who are seeking to unearth the knowledge of these ancient colossi.

So, be sure to check other titles from our *Esoteric Classics* series, as well as our *Occult Fiction, Theosophical Classics, Foundations of Freemasonry Series, Supernatural Fiction, Paranormal Research Series, Studies in Buddhism* and our *Christian Apocrypha Series*. You can also download the audio versions of most of these titles from Amazon, Apple or Audible, for learning on the go.

FUNDAMENTALS OF QABBALISTIC COSMOGONY

The Qabbalists conceive of the Supreme Deity as an Incomprehensible Principle to be discovered only through the process of eliminating, in order, all its cognizable attributes. That which remains--when every knowable thing has been removed--is AIN SOPH, the eternal state of *Being*. Although indefinable, the Absolute permeates all space. Abstract to the degree of inconceivability, AIN SOPH is the *unconditioned state of all things*. Substances, essences, and intelligences are manifested out of the inscrutability of AIN SOPH, but the Absolute itself is without substance, essence, or intelligence. AIN SOPH may be likened to a great field of rich earth out of which rises a myriad of plants, each different in color, formation, and fragrance, yet each with its roots in the same dark loam--which, however, is unlike any of the forms nurtured by it. The "plants" are universes, gods, and man, all nourished by AIN SOPH and all with their source in one definitionless essence; all with their spirits, souls, and bodies fashioned from this essence, and doomed, like the plant, to return to the black ground--AIN SOPH, the only Immortal--whence they came.

AIN SOPH was referred to by the Qabbalists as *The Most Ancient of all the Ancients*. It was always considered as sexless. Its symbol was a closed eye. While it may be truly said of AIN SOPH that to define It is to defile It, the Rabbis postulated certain theories regarding the manner in which AIN SOPH projected creations out of Itself, and they also assigned to this

Absolute Not-Being certain symbols as being descriptive, in part at least, of Its powers. The nature of AIN SOPH they symbolize by a circle, itself emblematic of eternity. This hypothetical circle encloses a dimensionless area of incomprehensible life, and the circular boundary of this life is abstract and measureless infinity.

According to this concept, God is not only a Center but also Area. Centralization is the first step towards limitation. Therefore, centers which form in the substances of AIN SOPH are finite because they are predestined to dissolution back into the Cause of themselves, while AIN SOPH Itself is infinite because It is the ultimate condition of all things. The circular shape given to AIN SOPH signifies that space is hypothetically enclosed within a great crystal-like globe, outside of which there is nothing, not even a vacuum. Within this globe--symbolic of AIN SOPH--creation and dissolution take place. Every element and principle that will ever be used in the eternities of Kosmic birth, growth, and decay is within the transparent substances of this intangible sphere. It is the Kosmic Egg which is not broken till the great day "Be With Us," which is the end of the Cycle of Necessity, when all things return to their ultimate cause.

In the process of creation the diffused life of AIN SOPH retires from the circumference to the center of the circle and establishes a point, which is the first manifesting One--the primitive limitation of the all-pervading O. When the Divine Essence thus retires from the circular boundary to the center,

It leaves behind the Abyss, or, as the Qabbalists term it, the Great Privation. Thus, in AIN SOPH is established a twofold condition where previously had existed but one. The first condition is the central point--the primitive objectified radiance of the eternal, subjectified life. About this radiance is darkness caused by the deprivation of the life which is drawn to the center to create the first point, or universal germ. The universal AIN SOPH, therefore, no longer shines through space, but rather upon space from an established first point. Isaac Myer describes this process as follows: "The Ain Soph at first was filling All and then made an absolute concentration into Itself which produced the Abyss, Deep, or Space, the Aveer Qadmon or Primitive Air, the Azoth; but this is not considered in the Qabbalah as a perfect void or vacuum, a perfectly empty Space, but is thought of as the Waters or Crystalline Chaotic Sea, in which was a certain degree of Light inferior to that by which all the created [worlds and hierarchies] were made." (See *The Qabbalah*.)

In the secret teachings of the Qabbalah it is taught that man's body is enveloped in an ovoid of bubble-like iridescence, which is called the Auric Egg. This is the causal sphere of man. It bears the same relationship to man's physical body that the globe of AIN SOPH bears to Its created universes. In fact, this Auric Egg is the AIN SOPH sphere of the entity called man. In reality, therefore, the supreme consciousness of man is in this aura, which extends in all directions and completely encircles his lower bodies. As the consciousness in the Kosmic Egg is withdrawn into a central point, which is then called God--the Supreme One--so the consciousness in the Auric Egg of

11

man is concentrated, thereby causing the establishment of a point of consciousness called the Ego. As the universes in Nature are formed from powers latent in the Kosmic Egg, so everything used by man in all his incarnations throughout the kingdoms of Nature is drawn from the latent powers within his Auric Egg. Man never passes from this egg; it remains even after death. His births, deaths, and rebirths all take place within it, and it cannot be broken until the lesser day "Be With Us," when mankind--like the universe--is liberated from the Wheel of Necessity.

THE QABBALISTIC SYSTEM OF WORLDS

On the accompanying circular chart, the concentric rings represent diagrammatically the forty rates of vibration (called by the Qabbalists Spheres) which emanate from AIN SOPH. The circle X 1 is the outer boundary of space. It circumscribes the area of AIN SOPH. The nature of AIN SOPH Itself is divided into three parts, represented by the spaces respectively between X 1 and X 2, X 2 and X 3, X 3 and A 1.[1]

It should be borne in mind that in the beginning the Supreme Substance, AIN, alone permeated the area of the circle; the inner rings had not yet come into manifestation. As the Divine Essence concentrated Itself, the rings X 2 and X 3 became apprehensible, for AIN SOPH is a limitation of AIN, and AIN SOPH AUR, or Light, is a still greater limitation. Thus the nature of the Supreme One is considered to be threefold, and from this threefold nature the powers and elements of creation were reflected into the Abyss left by the motion of AIN SOPH towards the center of Itself. The continual motion of AIN SOPH towards the center of Itself resulted in the establishment of the dot in the circle. The dot was called God,

---

[1] Thus:

X 1 to X 2,	אין,	AIN, the vacuum of pure spirit.
X 2 to X 3,	אין סוף,	AIN SOPH, the Limitless and Boundless.
X 3 to A 1,	אין סוף אור,	AIN SOPH AUR, the Limitless Light.

as being the supreme individualization of the Universal Essence. Concerning this the Zohar says:

"When the concealed of the Concealed wished to reveal Himself He first made a single point: the Infinite was entirely unknown, and diffused no light before this luminous point violently broke through into vision."

The name of this point is I AM, called by the Hebrews *Eheieh*. The Qabbalists gave many names to this dot. On this subject Christian D. Ginsberg writes, in substance: The dot is called the first crown, because it occupies the highest position. It is called the aged, because it is the first emanation. It is called the primordial or smooth point. It is called the white head, the *Long Face*--Macroprosophus--and the inscrutable height, because it controls and governs all the other emanations.

When the white shining point had appeared, it was called *Kether*, which means the *Crown*, and out of it radiated nine great globes, which arranged themselves in the form of a tree. These nine together with the first crown constituted the first system of *Sephiroth*. These ten were the first limitation of ten abstract points within the nature of AIN SOPH Itself. The power of AIN SOPH did not descend into these globes but rather was reflected upon them as the light of the sun is reflected upon the earth and planets. These ten globes were called the shining *sapphires*, and it is believed by many Rabbins that the word *sapphire* is the basis of the word *Sephira* (the

THE HEBREW TRIAD [2]

singular of Sephiroth). The great area which had been privated by the withdrawal of AIN SOPH into the central point, *Kether*, was now filled by four concentric globes called worlds, or spheres, and the light of the ten Sephiroth was reflected down through each of these in turn. This resulted in the establishment of four symbolical trees, each hearing the reflections of the ten Sephirothic globes. The 40 spheres of creation out of AIN SOPH are divided into four great world chains, as follows:

A 1 to A 10, *Atziluth*, the Boundless World of Divine Names.

B 1 to B 10, *Briah*, the Archangelic World of Creations.

---

[2] The Qabbalists used the letter שׁ, Shin, to signify the trinity of the first three Sephiroth. The central circle slightly above the other two is the first Sephira--*Kether*, the White Head, the Crown. The other two circles represent *Chochmah*, the Father, and *Binah*, the Mother. From the union of the Divine Father and the Divine Mother are produced the worlds and the generations of living things. The three flame-like points of the letter שׁ have long been used to conceal this Creative Triad of the Qabbalists.

C 1 to C 10, *Yetzirah*, the Hierarchal World of Formations.

D 1 to D 10, *Assiah*, the Elemental World of Substances.

Each of these worlds has ten powers, or spheres--a parent globe and nine others which conic out of it as emanations, each globe born out of the one preceding. On the plane of *Atziluth* (A 1 to A 10), the highest and most divine of all the created worlds, the unmanifested AIN SOPH established His first point or dot in the Divine Sea--the three spheres of X. This dot--A 1--contains all creation within it, but in this first divine and uncontaminated state the dot, or first manifested. God, was not considered as a personality by the Qabbalists but rather as a divine establishment or foundation. It was called the *First Crown* and from it issued the other circles of the *Atziluthic World*: A 2, A 3, A 4, A 5, A 6, A 7, A 8, A 9, and A 10. In the three lower worlds these circles are intelligences, planers, and elements, but in this first divine world they are called the *Rings of the Sacred Names*.

The first ten great circles (or globes) of light which were manifested out of AIN SOPH and the ten names of God assigned to them by the Qabbalists are as follows:

From AIN SOPH came A 1, the First Crown, and the name of the first power of God was *Eheieh*, which means *I Am* [*That I Am*].

From A 1 came A 2, the first Wisdom, and the name of the second power of God was *Jehovah*, which means *Essence of Being*.

From A 2 came A 3, the first Understanding, and the name of the third power of God was *Jehovah Elohim*, which means *God of Gods*.

From A 3 came A 4, the first Mercy, and the name of the fourth power of God was *El*, which means *God the Creator*.

From A 4 came A 5, the first Severity, and the name of the fifth power of God was *Elohim Gibor*, which means *God the Potent*.

From A 5 came A 6, the first Beauty, and the name of the sixth power of God was *Eloah Vadaath*, which means *God the Strong*.

From A 6 came A 7, the first Victory, and the name of the seventh power of God was *Jehovah Tzaboath*, which means *God of Hosts*.

From A 7 came A 8, the first Glory, and the name of the eighth power of God was *Elohim Tzaboath*, which means *Lord God of Hosts*.

From A 8 came A 9, the first Foundation, and the name of the ninth power of God was *Shaddai, El Chai*, which means *Omnipotent*.

From A 9 came A 10, the first Kingdom, and the name of the tenth power of God was *Adonai Melekh*, which means *God*.

From A 10 came B 1, the Second Crown, and the World of *Briah* was established.

The ten emanations from A 1 to A 10 inclusive are called the foundations of all creations. The Qabbalists designate them the ten roots of the Tree of Life. They are arranged in the form of a great human figure called Adam Qadmon--the man made from the fire mist (red dirt), the prototypic Universal Man. In the *Atziluthic* World, the powers of God are most purely manifested. These ten pure and perfect radiations do not descend into the lower worlds and take upon themselves forms, but are reflected upon the substances of the inferior spheres. From the first, or *Atziluthic*, World they are reflected into the second, or *Briatic*, World. As the reflection always lacks some of the brilliancy of the original image, so in the *Briatic* World the ten radiations lose part of their infinite power. A reflection is always like the thing reflected, but smaller and fainter.

In the second world, B 1 to B 10, the order of the spheres is the Name as in the *Atziluthic* World, but the ten circles of light are less brilliant and more tangible, and are here referred to as ten great Spirits--divine creatures who assist in the establishment of order and intelligence in the universe. As already noted, B 1 is born out of A 10 and is included within all the spheres superior to itself. Out of B 1 are taken nine globes--B 2, B 3, B 4, B 5, B 6, B 7, B 8, B 9, and B 10--which constitute the World of *Briah*. These ten subdivisions, however, are really the ten Atziluthic powers reflected into the substance of the *Briatic* World. B 1 is the ruler of this world, for it contains all the other rings of its own world and also the rings of the third and fourth worlds, C and D. In the World of *Briah* the ten spheres of light are called the *Archangels of Briah*. Their order and powers are as follows:

From A 10 came B 1, the Second Crown; it is called *Metatron*, the Angel of the Presence.

From B 1 came B 2, the second Wisdom; it is called *Raziel*, the Herald of Deity who revealed the mysteries of Qabbalah to Adam.

From B 2 carne B 3, the second Understanding; it is called *Tsaphkiel*, the Contemplation of God.

From B 3 came B 4, the second Mercy; it is called *Tsadkiel*, the justice of God.

From B 4 came B 5, the second Severity; it is called *Samael*, the Severity of God.

From B 5 came B 6, the second Beauty; it is called *Michael*, Like Unto God.

From B 6 came B 7, the second Victory; it is called *Haniel*, the Grace of God.

From B 7 came B 8, the second Glory; it is called *Raphael*, the Divine Physician.

From B 8 came B 9, the second Foundation; it is called *Gabriel*, the Man-God.

From B 9 came B 10, the second Kingdom; it is called *Sandalphon*, the Messias.

From B 10 came C 1, the Third Crown, and the World of *Yetzirah* was established.

The ten Archangels of *Briah* are conceived to be ten great spiritual beings, whose duty is to manifest the ten powers of the Great Name of God existent in the *Atziluthic* World, which surrounds and interpenetrates the entire world of creation. All things manifesting in the lower worlds exist first in the intangible rings of the upper spheres, so that creation is, in truth, the process of making tangible the intangible by extending the intangible into various vibratory rates. The ten globes of *Briatic* power, while themselves reflections, are mirrored downward into the third or *Yetziratic* World, where still more limited in their expression they become the spiritual and invisible zodiac which is behind the visible band of constellations. In this third world the ten globes of the original Atziluthic World are greatly limited and dimmed, but they are still infinitely powerful in comparison with the state of substance in which man dwells. In the third world, C 1 to C 10, the globes become hierarchies of celestial creatures, called the *Choirs of Yetzirah*. Here again, all are included within the ring C 1, the power which controls the Yetziratic World and which includes within itself and controls the entire world D. The order of the globes and the names of the hierarchies composing them are as follows:

From B 10 came C 1, the Third Crown; the Hierarchy is the Cherubim, *Chaioth Ha Kadosh*, the Holy Animals.

From C 1 came C 2, the third Wisdom; the Hierarchy is the Cherubim, *Orphanim*, the Wheels.

From C 2 came C 3, the third Understanding; the Hierarchy is the Thrones, *Aralim*, the Mighty Ones.

From C 3 came C 4, the third Mercy; the Hierarchy is the Dominations, *Chashmalim*, the Brilliant Ones.

From C 4 came C 5, the third Severity; the Hierarchy is the Powers, *Seraphim*, the Flaming Serpents.

From C 5 came C 6, the third Beauty; the Hierarchy is the Virtues, *Melachim*, the Kings.

From C 6 came C 7, the third Victory; the Hierarchy is the Principalities, *Elohim*, the Gods.

From C 7 came C 8, the third Glory; the Hierarchy is the Archangels, *Ben Elohim*, the Sons of God.

From C 8 came C 9, the third Foundation; the Hierarchy is the Angels, *Cherubim*, the Scat of the Sons.

From C 9 came C 10, the third Kingdom; the Hierarchy is Humanity, the *Ishim*, the Souls of Just Men.

From C 10 came D 1, the Fourth Crown, and the World of *Assiah* was established.

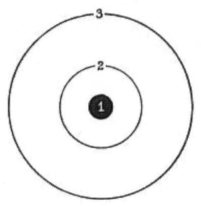

THE PLAN OF DIVINE ACTIVITY [3]

From the *Yetziratic* World the light of the ten spheres is reflected into the World of *Assiah*, the lowest of the four. The ten globes of the original *Atziluthic* World here take upon themselves forms of physical matter and the sidereal system is the result. The World of *Assiah*, or the elemental world of substance, is the one into which humanity descended at the time of Adam's fall. The Garden of Eden is the three upper worlds, and for his sins man was forced into the sphere of substance and assumed coats of skin (bodies). All of the

---

[3] According to the Qabbalists, the life of the Supreme Creator permeates all substance, all space, and all time, but for diagrammatic purposes the Supreme, All-Inclusive Life is limited by Circle 3, which may be called "the boundary line of Divine existence." The Divine Life permeating the area bounded by Circle 3 is focused at Point 1, which thus becomes the personification of the impersonal life and is termed "the First Crown." The creative forces pouring through Point 1 come into manifestation as the objective universe in the intermediate space, Circle 2.

spiritual forces of the upper worlds, A, B, C, when they strike against the elements of the lower world, D, are distorted and perverted, resulting in the creation of hierarchies of demons to correspond with the good spirits in each of the higher worlds. In all the ancient Mysteries, matter was regarded as the source of all evil and spirit the source of all good, for matter inhibits and limits, often so clogging the inner perceptions that man is unable to recognize his own divine potentialities. Since matter thus prevents humanity from claiming its birthright, it is called the Adversary, the power of evil. The fourth world, D, is the world of solar systems, comprising not only the one of which the earth is a part but all the solar systems in the universe.

Opinions differ as to the arrangement of the globes of this last world, D 1 to D 10 inclusive. The ruler of the fourth world is D 1, called by some the *Fiery Heaven*; by others the *Primum Mobile*, or the *First Motion*. From this whirling fire emanates the material starry zodiac, D 2, in contradistinction to the invisible spiritual zodiac of the *Yetziratic* World. From the zodiac, D 2, are differentiated the spheres of the planets in concatenate order. The ten spheres of the World of *Assiah* are as follows:

From C 10 came D 1, the Fourth Crown; *Rashith Ha-Galagalum*, the *Primum Mobile*, the fiery mist which is the beginning of the material universe.

From D 1 came D 2, the fourth Wisdom; *Masloth*, the Zodiac, the Firmament of the Fixed Stars.

From D 2 came D 3, the fourth Understanding; *Shabbathai*, the sphere of Saturn.

From D 3 came D 4, the fourth Mercy; *Tzedeg*, the sphere of Jupiter.

From D 4 came D 5, the fourth Severity; *Madim*, the sphere of Mars.

From D 5 came D 6, the fourth Beauty; *Shemesh*, the sphere of the Sun.

From D 6 came D 7, the fourth Victory; *Nogah*, the sphere of Venus.

From D 7 came D 8, the fourth Glory; *Kokab*, the sphere of Mercury.

From D 8 came D 9, the fourth Foundation; *Levanah*, the sphere of the Moon.

From D 9 came D 10, the Fourth Kingdom; *Cholom Yosodoth*, the sphere of the Four Elements.

By inserting a sphere (which he calls the Empyrean) before the Primum Mobile, Kircher moves each of the other spheres down one, resulting in the elimination of the sphere of the elements and making D 10 the sphere of the Moon.

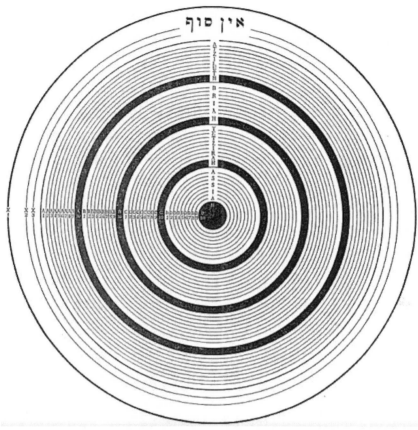

THE QABBALISTIC SCHEME OF THE FOUR WORLDS [4]

---

[4] In the above chart the dark line between X 3 and A 1 constitutes the boundary of the original dot, while the concentric circles within this heavier line symbolize the emanations and the worlds which came forth from the dot. As this dot is contained within the outer rings X 1, X 2, and X 3, and represents the first establishment of an individualized existence, so the lower universe symbolized by the forty concentric circles within the dot represents the lower creation evolved out of and yet contained within the nature of the first Crown, which may be called God, within whom the divine powers, the celestial beings the sidereal worlds, and man, live and move and have their being. It is highly important that all the rings within A 1 be considered as being enclosed by the primitive dot, which is itself encircled by the great ring X 1, or the Auric Egg of AIN SOPH.

Each ring includes within its own nature all the rings within itself and is included within the natures of all the rings outside of itself. Thus, A 1--the primitive dot--controls and contains the thirty-nine rings which it encloses, all of these partaking of its nature in varying degrees according to their respective dignities. Consequently, the entire area from A 1 to D 10 inclusive is the original dot, and the rings symbolize the divisions which took place with in it and the emanations which poured out from it after its establishment in the midst of the abstract nature of AIN SOPH. The powers of the rings decrease towards the center of the diagram, for Power is measured by the number of things controlled, and each ring controls the rings within it and is controlled by the rings outside of it. Thus, while A 1 controls thirty-nine rings besides itself,

In the World of *Assiah* are to be found the demons and tempters. These are likewise reflections of the ten great globes of *Atziluth*, but because of the distortion of the images resulting from the base substances of the World of *Assiah* upon which they are reflected, they become evil creatures, called *shells* by the Qabbalists. There are ten hierarchies of these demons to correlate with the ten hierarchies of good spirits composing the *Yetziratic* World. There are also ten Archdemons, corresponding to the ten Archangels of *Briah*. The black magicians use these inverted spirits in their efforts to attain their nefarious ends, but in time the demon destroys those who bind themselves to it. The ten orders of demons and the ten Archdemons of the World of *Assiah* are as follows:

D 1, the evil Crown; the hierarchy is called *Thaumiel*, the doubles of God, the Two-headed; the Archdemons are *Satan* and *Moloch*.

From D 1 came D 2, the evil Wisdom; the hierarchy is called *Chaigidiel*, those who obstruct; the Archdemon is *Adam Belial*.

B 1 controls only twenty-nine rings besides its own. Therefore, A 1 is more powerful than B 1. As the greatest spiritual solidity, or permanence, is at the circumference and the greatest material density, or impermanence, is at the center of the diagram, the rings as they decrease in Power become more material and substantial until the center sphere, D 10, symbolizes the actual chemical elements of the earth. The rates of vibration are also lower as the rings approach the center. Thus, the vibration of A 2 is lower than A 1 but higher than A 3, and so on in decreasing scale towards the center, A 1 being the highest and D 10 the lowest sphere of creation. While A 1, the ruler of creation, controls the circles marked A, B, C, and D, it is less than the three rings of AIN SOPH--X 1, X2, and X3--and therefore bows before the throne of the ineffable Creator from whose substances it was individualized.

From D 2 came D 3, the evil Understanding; the hierarchy is called *Satharial*, the concealment of God, the Archdemon is *Lucifuge*.

From D 3 came D 4, the evil Mercy; the hierarchy is called *Gamchicoth*, the disturber of things; the Archdemon is *Astaroth*.

From D 4 came D 5, the evil Severity; the hierarchy is called *Golab*, incendiarism and burning; the Archdemon is *Asmodeus*.

From D 5 came D 6, the evil Beauty; the hierarchy is called *Togarini*, the wranglers; the Archdemon is *Belphegor*.

From D 6 came D 7, the evil Victory; the hierarchy is called *Harab Serap*, the dispensing Raven; the Archdemon is *Baal Chanan*.

From D 7 came D 8, the evil Glory; the hierarchy is called *Samael*, the embroiler; the Archdemon is *Adramelek*.

From D 8 came D 9, the evil Foundation; the hierarchy is called *Gamaliel*, the obscene; the Archdemon is *Lilith*.

From D 9 came D 10, the evil Kingdom; the hierarchy is called *Nahemoth*, the impure; the Archdemon is *Nahema*.

The Qabbalists declare that the worlds, intelligences, and hierarchies were established according to the vision of Ezekiel.

By the man of Ezekiel's vision is symbolized the World of *Atziluth*; by the throne, the World of *Briah*; by the firmament, the World of *Yetzirah*; and by the living creatures the World of *Assiah*. These spheres are the wheels within wheels of the prophet. The Qabbalists next established a human figure in each of the four worlds: A 1 was the head and A 10 the feet of the man of *Atziluth*; B 1 was the head and B 10 the feet of the man of *Briah*; C 1 was the head and C 10 the feet of the man of *Yetzirah*; D 1 was the head and D 10 the feet of the man of *Assiah*. These four are called the *World Men*. They are considered androgynous and are the prototypes of humanity.

The human body, like that of the universe, is considered to be a material expression of ten globes or spheres of light. Therefore man is called the Microcosm--the little world, built in the image of the great world of which he is a part. The Qabbalists also established a mysterious universal man with his head at A 1 and his feet at D 10. This is probably the secret significance of the great figure of Nebuchadnezzar's dream, with its head in the World of *Atziluth*, its arms and hands in the World of *Briah*, its generative system in the World of *Yetzirah*, and its legs and feet in the World of *Assiah*. This is the *Grand Man of the Zohar*, of whom Eliphas Levi writes:

"It is not less astonishing to observe at the beginning of the Zohar the profundity of its notions and the sublime simplicity of its images. It is said as follows: 'The science of equilibrium is the key of occult science. Unbalanced forces perish in the void. So passed the kings of the elder world, the princes of the giants.

They have fallen like trees without roots, and their place is found no more. Through the conflict of unbalanced forces, the devastated earth was void and formless, until the Spirit of God made for itself a place in heaven and reduced the mass of waters. All the aspirations of Nature were directed then towards unity of form, towards the living synthesis (if equilibrated forces; the face of God, crowned with light, rose over the vast sea and was reflected in the waters thereof. His two eyes were manifested, radiating with splendour, darting two beams of light which crossed with those of the reflection. The brow of God and His eyes formed a triangle in heaven, and its reflection formed a second triangle in the waters. So was revealed the number six, being that of universal creation.' The text, which would be unintelligible in a literal version, is translated here by way of interpretation. The author makes it plain that the human form which he ascribes to Deity is only an image of his meaning and that God is beyond expression by human thought or representation by any figure. Pascal said that God is a circle, of which the center is everywhere and the circumference nowhere. But how is one to imagine a circle apart from its circumference? The Zohar adopts the antithesis of this paradoxical image and in respect of the circle of Pascal would say rather that the circumference is everywhere, while that which is nowhere is the center. It is however to a balance and not to a circle that it compares the universal equilibrium of things. It affirms that equilibrium is everywhere and so also is the central point where the balance hangs in suspension. We find that the Zohar is thus more forcible and more profound than Pascal. * * * The Zohar is a genesis of light; the Sepher Yetzirah is a ladder of truth. Therein are expounded the two-

and-thirty absolute symbols of speech--being numbers and letters. Each letter produces a number, an idea and a form, so that mathematics are applicable to forms and ideas, even as to numbers, in virtue of an exact proportion, and a perfect correspondence. By the science of the Sepher Yetzirah, the human mind is rooted in truth and in reason; it accounts for all progress possible to intelligence by means of the evolution of numbers. Thus does the Zohar represent absolute truth, while the Sepher Yetzirah furnishes the method of its acquisition, its discernment and application." (*History of Magic.*)

By placing man himself at the point D 10, his true constitution is revealed. He exists upon four worlds, only one of which is visible. It is then made evident that his parts and members upon the material plane are, by analogy, hierarchies and intelligences in the higher worlds. Here, again, the law of interpenetration is evidenced. Although within man is the entire universe (the 43 spheres interpenetrating D 10), he is ignorant of its existence because he cannot exercise control over that which is superior to or greater than himself. Nevertheless, all these higher spheres exercise control over him, as his functions and activities demonstrate. If they did not, he would be an inert mass of substance. Death is merely the result of deflecting the life impulses of the higher rings away from the lower body.

The control of the transubstantial rings over their own material reflection is called *life*, and the spirit of man is, in reality, a name given to this great host of intelligences, which are focused upon substance through a point called the *ego*, established in the midst of themselves. X 1 is the outside boundary of the human Auric Egg, and the entire diagram becomes a cross section of the constitution of man, or a cross section of the Kosmic constitution, if correlated with the universe. By the secret culture of the Qabbalistic School, man is taught how to climb the rings (unfold his consciousness) until at last he returns to AIN SOPH. The process by which this is accomplished is called the *Fifty Gates of Light*. Kircher, the Jesuit Qabbalist, declares that Moses passed through forty-nine of the gates, but that Christ alone passed the fiftieth gate.

To the third edition of the *Sepher Yetzirah* translated from the Hebrew by Wm. Wynn Westcott are appended the Fifty Gates of Intelligence emanating from *Binah*, the second Sephira. The source of this information is Kircher's *Œdipus Ægyptiacus*. The gates are divided into six orders, of which the first four have each ten subdivisions, the fifth nine, and the sixth only one.

The first order of gates is termed *Elementary* and its divisions areas follows: (1) Chaos, Hyle, the First Matter; (2) Formless, void, lifeless; (3) The Abyss; (4) Origin of the Elements; (5) Earth (no seed germs); (6) Water;(7) Air;(8) Fire;(9) Differentiation of qualities; (10) Mixture and combination.

The second order of gates is termed *Decad of Evolution* and its divisions areas follows: (11) Minerals differentiate; (12) Vegetable principles appear; (13) Seeds germinate in moisture; (14) Herbs and Trees; (15) Fructification in vegetable life; (16)

Origin of low forms of animal life; (17) Insects and Reptiles appear; (18) Fishes, vertebrate life in the waters; (19) Birds, vertebrate life in the air; (20) Quadrupeds, vertebrate earth animals.

The third order of gates is termed *Decad of Humanity* and its divisions are as follows: (21) Appearance of Man; (22) Material human body; (23) Human Soul conferred; (24) Mystery of Adam and Eve; (25) Complete Man as the Microcosm; (26) Gift of five human faces acting exteriorly; (27) Gift of five powers to the soul; (28) Adam Kadmon, the Heavenly Man; (29) Angelic beings, (30) Man in the image of God.

The fourth order of gates is termed *World of Spheres* and its divisions are as follows: (31) The Heaven of the Moon; (32) The Heaven of Mercury, (33) The Heaven of Venus; (34) The Heaven of the Sun; (35) The Heaven of Mars; (36) The Heaven of Jupiter; (37) The Heaven of Saturn; (38) The Firmament; (39) The Primum Mobile; (40) The Empyrean Heaven.

The fifth order of gates is termed *The Angelic World* and its divisions are as follows: (41) Ishim--Sons of Fire; (42) Orphanim--Cherubim; (43) Aralim--Thrones; (44) Chashmalim--Dominions; (45) Seraphim--Virtues; (46) Melachim--Powers; (47) Elohim--Principalities; (48) Ben Elohim--Angels; (49) Cherubim--Archangels. [The order of the Angels is a matter of controversy, the arrangement above differing from that accepted in other sections of this volume. The Rabbins disagree fundamentally as to the proper sequence of the Angelic names.]

The sixth order is termed *The Archetype* and consists of but one gate: (50) God, AIN SOPH, He whom no mortal eye hath seen. The fiftieth gate leads from creation into the Creative Principle and he who passes through it returns into the unlimited and undifferentiated condition of ALL. The fifty gates reveal a certain evolutionary process and it was declared by the Rabbins that he who would attain to the highest degree of understanding must pass sequentially through all of these orders of life, each of which constituted a gate in that the spirit, passing from the lower to the higher, found in each more responsive organism new avenues of self-expression.

THE TREE OF THE SEPHIROTH

The Tree of the Sephiroth may be considered an invaluable compendium of the secret philosophy which originally was the spirit and soul of Chasidism. The Qabbalah is the priceless heritage of Israel, but each year those who comprehend its true principles become fewer in number. The Jew of today, if he lacks a realization of the profundity of his people's doctrines, is usually permeated with that most dangerous form of ignorance, modernism, and is prone to regard the Qabbalah either as an evil to be shunned like the plague or as a ridiculous superstition which has survived the black magic of the Dark Ages. Yet without the key which the Qabbalah supplies, the spiritual mysteries of both the Old and the New Testament must remain unsolved by Jew and Gentile alike.

The Sephirothic Tree consists of ten globes of luminous splendor arranged in three vertical columns and connected by 22 channels or paths. The ten globes are called the *Sephiroth* and to them are assigned the numbers i to 10. The three columns are called *Mercy* (on the right), *Severity* (on the left), and, between them, *Mildness*, as the reconciling power. The columns may also be said to represent *Wisdom*, *Strength*, and *Beauty*, which form the triune support of the universe, for it is written that the foundation of all things is the *Three*. The 22 channels are the letters of the Hebrew alphabet and to them are assigned the major trumps of the Tarot deck of symbolic cards.

Eliphas Levi declared that by arranging the Tarot cards according to a definite order man could discover all that is knowable concerning his God, his universe, and himself. When the ten numbers which pertain to the globes (Sephiroth) are combined with the 22 letters relating to the channels, the resultant sum is 32--the number peculiar to the Qabbalistic Paths of Wisdom. These Paths, occasionally referred to as the 32 teeth in the mouth of the *Vast Countenance* or as the 32 nerves that branch out from the Divine Brain, are analogous to the first 32 degrees of Freemasonry, which elevate the candidate to the dignity of a Prince of the Royal Secret. Qabbalists also consider it extremely significant that in the original Hebrew Scriptures the name of God should occur 32 times in the first chapter of Genesis. (In the English translations of the Bible the name appears 33 times.) In the mystic analysis of the human body, according to the Rabbins, 32 spinal segments lead upward to the Temple of Wisdom--the skull.

The four Qabbalistic Trees described in the preceding chapter were combined by later Jewish scholars into one all-inclusive diagram and termed by them not only the Sephirothic but also the *Archetypal*, or *Heavenly, Adam*. According to some authorities, it is this Heavenly Adam, and not a terrestrial man, whose creation is described in the opening chapters of Genesis. Out of the substances of this divine man the universe was formed; in him it remains and will continue even after dissolution shall resolve the spheres back into their own primitive substance. The Deity is never conceived of as actually contained in the Sephiroth, which are purely hypothetical vessels employed to define the limits of the Creative Essence. Adolph Franck rather likens the Sephiroth to varicolored transparent glass bowls filled with pure light, which apparently assumes the color of its containers but whose essential nature remains ever unchanged and unchangeable.

The ten Sephiroth composing the body of the prototypic Adam, the numbers related to them, and the parts of the universe to which they correspond are as follows:

No.	SEPHIROTH	THE UNIVERSE	ALTERNATIVE
1	Kether--the Crown	Primum Mobile	The Fiery Heavens
2	Chochmah--Wisdom	The Zodiac	The First Motion
3	Binah--Understanding	Saturn	The Zodiac
4	Chesed--Mercy	Jupiter	Saturn
5	Geburah--Severity	Mars	Jupiter
6	Tiphereth--Beauty	Sun	Mars
7	Netsah--Victory	Venus	Sun
8	Hod--Glory	Mercury	Venus
9	Jesod--the Foundation	Moon	Mercury
10	Malchuth--the Kingdom	Elements	Moon

It must continually be emphasized that the Sephiroth and the properties assigned to them, like the tetractys of the Pythagoreans, are merely symbols of the cosmic system with its multitude of parts. The truer and fuller meaning of these emblems may not be revealed by writing or by word of mouth, but must be divined as the result of study and meditation. In the *Sepher ha Zohar* it is written that there is a *garment*--the written doctrine-which every man may see. Those with understanding do not look upon the *garment* but at the body beneath it--the intellectual and philosophical code. The wisest of all, however, the servants of the Heavenly King, look at nothing save the soul--the spiritual doctrine--which is the eternal and ever-springing root of the law. Of this great truth Eliphas Levi also writes declaring that none can gain entrance to the secret House of Wisdom unless he wear the voluminous *cape* of Apollonius of Tyana and carry in his hand the *lamp* of Hermes. The cape signifies the qualities of self-possession and self-reliance which must envelope the seeker as a cloak of strength, while the ever-burning lamp of the sage represents the illumined mind and perfectly balanced intellect without which the mystery of the ages can never be solved.

The Sephirothic Tree is sometimes depicted as a human body, thus more definitely establishing the true identity of the first, or Heavenly, Man--*Adam Kadmon*--the *Idea* of the Universe. The ten divine globes (Sephiroth) are then considered as analogous to the ten sacred members and organs of the *Protogonos*, according to the following arrangement. Kether is the crown of the Prototypic Head and perhaps refers to the pineal gland; Chochmah and Binah are the right and left hemispheres respectively of the Great Brain; Chesed and Geburah (Pechad) are the right and left arms respectively, signifying the active creative members of the Grand Man; Tiphereth is the heart, or, according to some, the entire viscera; Netsah and Hod are the right and left legs respectively, or the supports of the world; Jesod is the generative system, or the foundation of form; and Malchuth represents the two feet, or the base of being. Occasionally Jesod is considered as the male and Malchuth as the female generative power. The Grand Man thus conceived is the gigantic image of Nebuchadnezzar's dream, with head of gold, arms and chest of silver, body of brass, legs of iron, and feet of clay. The mediæval Qabbalists also assigned one of the Ten Commandments and a tenth part of the Lord's Prayer in sequential order to each of the ten Sephiroth.

Concerning the emanations from Kether which establish themselves as three triads of Creative Powers--termed in the *Sepher ha Zohar* three heads each with three faces--H. P. Blavatsky writes: "This [Kether] was the first Sephiroth, containing in herself the other nine ספירות Sephiroth, or intelligences. In their totality and unity they represent the archetypal man, *Adam Kadmon*, the πρωτόγονος, who in his individuality or unity is yet dual, or bisexual, the Greek *Didumos*, for he is the prototype of all humanity. Thus we obtain three trinities, each contained in a 'head.' In the first head, or face (the three-faced Hindu Trimurti), we find *Sephira* [Kether], the first androgyne, at the apex of the upper triangle, emitting *Hachama* [Chochmah], or Wisdom, a masculine and active potency--also called Jah, י"ה--and *Binah*, בינה, or Intelligence, a female and passive potency, also represented by the name Jehovah יהוה. These three form the first trinity or 'face' of the Sephiroth. This triad emanated *Hesed*, הסד, or Mercy, a masculine active potency, also called *El*, from which emanated *Geburah* גבורה, or justice, also called Eloha, a feminine passive potency; from the union of these two was

39

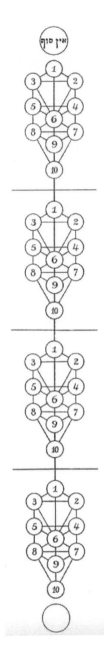

⁵ produced *Tiphereth* תפארת, Beauty, Clemency the Spiritual Sun, known by the divine name *Elohim*; and the second triad, 'face,' or 'head,' was formed. These emanating, in their turn, the masculine potency *Netzah*, נצה, Firmness, or Jehovah Sabaoth, who issued the feminine passive potency Hod, הוד, Splendor, or Elohim Sabaoth; the two produced *Jesod*, יסוד, Foundation, who is the mighty living one *El-Chai*, thus yielding the third trinity or 'head.' The tenth Sephiroth is rather a duad, and is represented on the diagrams as the lowest circle. It is *Malchuth* or Kingdom, מלכות, and *Shekinah*, שכינה, also called Adonai, and *Cherubim* among the angelic hosts. The first 'Head' is called the Intellectual world; the second 'Head' is the Sensuous, or the world of Perception, and the third is the material or Physical world." (See *Isis Unveiled.*)

Among the later Qabbalists there is also a division of the Sephirothic Tree into five parts, in which the distribution of the globes is according to the following order:

---

⁵ Depiction of the FOUR SEPHIROTHIC TREES. The forty concentric circles shown in the large circular cut in the preceding chapter are here arranged as four trees, each consisting of ten circles. These trees disclose the organization of the hierarchies controlling the destinies of all creation. The trees are the same in each of the four world but the powers vested in the globes express themselves differently through the substances of each world, resulting in endless differentiation.

(1) *Macroprosophus*, or the *Great Face*, is the term applied to Kether as the first and most exalted of the Sephiroth and includes the nine potencies or Sephiroth issuing from Kether.

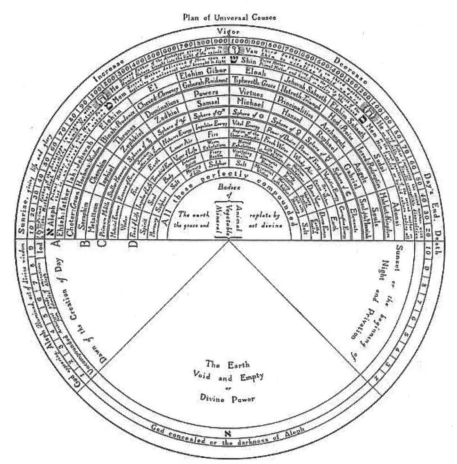

A TABLE OF SEPHIROTHIC CORRESPONDENCES [6]
From Fludd's *Collectio Operum*

---

[6] The above diagram has been specially translated from the Latin as being of unique value to students of Qabbalism and also as an example of Robert Fludd's unusual ability in assembling tables of correspondences. Robert Fludd ranks among the most eminent Rosicrucians and Freemasons; in fact, he has often been called "the first English Rosicrucian." He has written several valuable documents directly bearing upon the Rosicrucian enigma. It is significant that the most important of his works should be published at the same time as those of Bacon, Shakespeare, and the first Rosicrucian authors.

(2) *Abba*, the *Great Father*, is the term generally applied to Chochmah--Universal Wisdom--the first emanation of Kether, but, according to Ibn Gebirol, Chochmah represents the Son, the Logos or the Word born from the union of Kether and Binah.

(3) *Aima*, the *Great Mother*, is the name by which Binah, or the third Sephira, is generally known. This is the Holy Ghost, from whose body the generations issue forth. Being the third person of the Creative Triad, it corresponds to Jehovah, the Demiurgus.

(4) *Microprosophus*, or the *Lesser Face*, is composed of the six Sephiroth--Chesed, Geburah, Tiphereth, Netsah, Hod, and Jesod. The Microprosophus is commonly called the *Lesser Adam*, or *Zauir Anpin*, whereas the *Macroprosophus*, or *Superior Adam*, is *Arikh Anpin*. The Lesser Face is properly symbolized by the six-pointed star or interlaced triangles of Zion and also by the six faces of the cube. It represents the directions north, east, south, west, up, and down, and also the first six days of Creation. In his list of the parts of the Microprosophus, MacGregor-Mathers includes Binah as the first and superior part of the *Lesser Adam*, thus making his constitution septenary. If Microprosophus be considered as sexpartite, then his globes (Sephiroth) are analogous to the six days of Creation, and the tenth globe, Malchuth, to the Sabbath of rest.

(5) The Bride of *Microprosophus* is Malchuth--the epitome of the Sephiroth, its quaternary constitution being composed of blendings of the four elements. This is the divine Eve that is

taken out of the side of *Microprosophus* and combines the potencies of the entire Qabbalistic Tree in one sphere, which may be termed man.

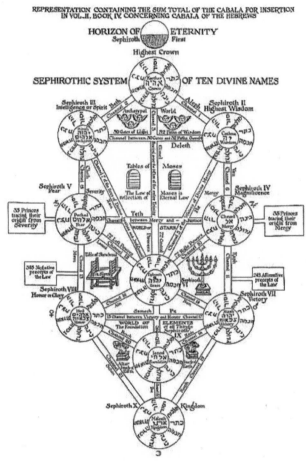

THE SEPHIROTHIC TREE OF THE LATER QABBALISTS
Translated from Kircher's *Œdipus Ægyptiacus* [7]

---

[7] Having demonstrated that the Qabbalists divided the universe into four worlds, each consisting of ten spheres, it is necessary to consider next how the ten spheres of each world were arranged into what is called the "Sephirothic Tree." This Tree is composed of ten circles, representing the numbers 1 to 20 and connected together by twenty-two canals--the twenty-two letters of the Hebrew alphabet. The ten numbers plus the twenty-two letters result in the occult number 32, which, according to the *Mishna*, signifies the Thirty-two Paths of Wisdom. Letters and numbers, according to the Qabbalists, are the keys to all knowledge, for by a secret system of arranging them the mysteries of creation are revealed. For this reason they are called

According to the mysteries of the Sephiroth, the order of the Creation, or the Divine Lightning Flash which zigzags through the four worlds according to the order of the divine emanations, is thus described: From AIN SOPH, the Nothing and All, the Eternal and Unconditioned Potency, issues *Macroprosophus*, the *Long Face*, of whom it is written, "Within His skull exist daily thirteen thousand myriads of worlds which draw their existence from Him and by Him are upheld." (See The Greater Holy Assembly.) *Macroprosophus*, the directionalized will of AIN SOPH, corresponding to Kether, the Crown of the Sephiroth, gives birth out of Himself to the nine lesser spheres of which He is the sum and the overbrooding cause. The 22 letters of the Hebrew alphabet, by the various combinations of which the laws of the universe are established, constitute the scepter of *Macroprosophus* which He wields from His flaming throne in the Atziluthic World.

From this eternal and ancient androgyne--Kether--come forth Chochmah, the great Father, and Binah, the great Mother. These two are usually referred to as Abba and Aima respectively--the first male and the first female, the prototypes of sex. These correspond to the first two letters of the sacred

---

"the Paths of Wisdom." This occult fact is carefully concealed in the 32nd degree of Freemasonry.

There are four trees, one in each of the four worlds established in the preceding chapter. The first is in the Atziluthic World, the ten circles being the ten globes of light established in the midst of AIN SOPH. The powers and attributes of this Tree are reflected into each of the three lower worlds, the form of the Tree remaining the same but its power diminishing as it descends. To further complicate their doctrine, the Qabbalists created another tree, which was a composite of all four of the world trees but consisted of only ten globes. In this single tree were condensed all the arcana previously scattered through the voluminous archives of Qabbalistic literature.

name, Jehovah, יהוה, *IHVH*. The Father is the י, or *I*, and the Mother is the ה, or *H*. *Abba* and *Aima* symbolize the creative activities of the universe, and are established in the creative world of Briah. In the *Sepher ha Zohar* it is written, "And therefore are all things established in the equality of male and female; for were it not so, how could they subsist? This beginning is the Father of all things; the Father of all Fathers; and both are mutually bound together, and the one path shineth into the other--Chochmah, Wisdom, as the Father; Binah, Understanding, as the Mother."

There is a difference of opinion concerning certain of the relationships of the parts of the first triad. Some Qabbalists, including Ibn Gebirol, consider Kether as the Father, Binah as the Mother, and Chochmah as the Son. In this later arrangement, Wisdom, which is the attribute of the Son, becomes the creator of the lower spheres. The symbol of Binah is the dove, a proper emblem for the brooding maternal instinct of the Universal Mother.

Because of the close similarity of their creative triad to the Christian Trinity, the later Qabbalists rearranged the first three Sephiroth and added a mysterious point called *Daath*--a hypothetical eleventh Sephira. This located where the horizontal line connecting Chochmah and Binah crosses the vertical line joining Kether and Tiphereth. While *Daath* is not mentioned by the first Qabbalists, it is a highly important element and its addition to the Sephirothic Tree was not made without full realization of the significance of such action. If Chochmah be considered the active, intelligent energy of

Kether, and Binah the receptive capacity of Kether, then *Daath* becomes the *thought* which, created by Chochmah, flows into Binah. The postulation of *Daath* clarifies the problem of the Creative Trinity, for here it is diagrammatically represented as consisting of Chochmah (the Father), Binah (the Mother, or Holy Ghost), and *Daath*, the Word by which the worlds were established. Isaac Myer discounts the importance of *Daath*, declaring it a subterfuge to conceal the fact that Kether, and not Chochmah; is the true Father of the Creative Triad. He makes no attempt to give a satisfactory explanation for the symbolism of this hypothetical Sephira.

According to the original conception, from the union of the Divine Father and the Divine Mother is produced *Microprosophus*--the *Short Face* or the *Lesser Countenance*, which is established in the Yetziratic World of formation and corresponds to the letter ו, or *V*, in the Great Name. The six powers of *Microprosophus* flow from and are contained in their own source, which is Binah, the Mother of the *Lesser Adam*. These constitute the spheres of the sacred planets; their name is Elohim, and they move upon the face of the deep. The tenth Sephira--Malchuth, the Kingdom--is described as the Bride of the *Lesser Adam*, created back to back with her lord, and to it is assigned the final, ה, or *H*, the last letter of the Sacred Name. The dwelling place of Malchuth is in the fourth world--Assiah--and it is composed of all the superior powers reflected into the elements of the terrestrial sphere. Thus it will be seen that the Qabbalistic Tree extends through four worlds, with its branches in matter and its roots in the Ancient of Ancients--*Macroprosophus*.

Three vertical columns support the universal system as typified by the Sephirothic Tree. The central pillar has its foundation in Kether, the Eternal One. It passes downward through the hypothetical Sephira, *Daath*, and then through Tiphereth and Jesod, with its lower end resting upon the firm foundation of Malchuth, the last of the globes. The true import of the central pillar is equilibrium. It demonstrates how the Deity always manifests by emanating poles of expression from the midst of Itself but remaining free from the illusion of polarity. If the numbers of the four Sephiroth connected by this column be added together (1 +6 +9 + 10), the sum is 26, the number of Jehovah. (See chapter on *Pythagorean Mathematics*.)

The column on the right, which is called *Jachin*, has its foundation on Chochmah, the outpouring Wisdom of God; the three globes suspended from it are all masculine potencies. The column at the left is called *Boaz*. The three globes upon it are feminine and receptive potencies, for it is founded in *Understanding*, a receptive and maternal potency. *Wisdom*, it will be noted, is considered as radiant or outpouring, and *Understanding* as receptive, or something which is filled by the flowing of *Wisdom*. The three pillars are ultimately united in Malchuth, in which all the powers of the superior worlds are manifested.

The four globes upon the central column reveal the function of the creative power in the various worlds. In the first world the creative power is *Will*--the one Divine Cause; in the second world, the hypothetical *Daath*--the Word coming forth from the Divine Thought; in the third world, Tiphereth--the Sun, or focal point between God and Nature; in the fourth world it is twofold, being the positive and negative poles of the reproductive system, of which Jesod is the male and Malchuth the female.

In Kircher's Sephirothic Tree it should be especially noted that the ornaments of the Tabernacle appear in the various parts of the diagram. These indicate a direct relationship between the sacred House of God and the universe--a relationship which must always be considered as existing between the Deity through whose activity the world is produced and the world itself, which must be the house or vehicle of that Deity. Could the modern scientific world but sense the true profundity of these philosophical deductions of the ancients, it would realize that those who fabricated the structure of the Qabbalah possessed a knowledge of the celestial plan comparable in every respect with that of the modern savant.

The *Tetragrammaton*, or the four-lettered Name of God, written thus יהוה, is pronounce Jehovah. The first letter is י, *Yod*, the Germ, the Life, the Flame, the Cause, the One, and the most fundamental of the Jewish phallic emblems. Its numerical value is 10, and it is to be considered as the 1 containing the 10. In the Qabbalah it is declared that the a *Yod* is in reality three *Yods*, of which the first is the *beginning*, the second is the *center*, and the third is the *end*. Its throne is the Sephira Chochmah (according to Ibn Gebirol, Kether), from which it goes forth to impregnate Binah, which is the first ה, *He*. The result of this union is Tiphereth, which is the ו *Vau*, whose power is 6 and which symbolizes the six members of the *Lesser Adam*. The final ה, *He*, is Malchuth, the *Inferior Mother*, partaking in part of the potencies of the *Divine Mother*, the first *He*. By placing the four letters of the *Tetragrammaton* in a vertical column, a figure closely resembling the human body is produced, with *Yod* for the head, the first *He* for the arms and shoulders, *Vau* for the trunk of the body, and the final *He* for the hips and legs. If the Hebrew letters be exchanged for their English equivalents, the form is not materially changed or the analogy altered. It is also extremely significant that by inserting the letter ש, *Shin*, in the middle of the name *Jehovah*, the word *Jehoshua*, or *Jesus*, is formed thus: יהשוה

In the Qabbalistic Mysteries, according to Eliphas Levi, the name *Jehovah* is occasionally written by connecting together 24 dots--the 24 powers before the throne--and it is believed that the name of the Power of Evil is the sign of Jehovah reversed or inverted. (See *Transcendental Magic*.) Of the Great Word, Albert Pike writes: "The True Word of a Mason is to be found in the concealed and profound meaning of the Ineffable Name of Deity, communicated by God to Moses; and which meaning was long lost by the very precautions taken to conceal it. The true pronunciation of that name was in truth a secret, in which, however, was involved the far more profound secret of its meaning. In that meaning is included all the truth that can be known by us, in regard to the nature of God." (See *Morals and Dogma*.)

Table of the SEPHIROTHS in Circles.

THE SEPHIROTH IN THE FORM OF THE SOLAR SYSTEM [8]
From Maurice's *Indian Antiquities*

---

[8] Thomas Maurice reproduces the above engraving, which is modification of the elaborate tree on the preceding page. The Sephiroth are here superimposed, decreasing in size as they decrease in power and dignity. Thus, the Crown is the greatest and the all-inclusive, and the Kingdom--which represents the physical universe--is the smallest and of least importance.

QABBALISTIC KEYS TO THE
CREATION OF MAN

Henrie Stephen, in *A World of Wonders*, published in 1607, mentions a monk of St. Anthony who declared that while in Jerusalem the patriarch of that city had shown him not only one of the ribs of the *Word made flesh* and some rays from the Star of Bethlehem, but also the snout of a seraph, a finger nail of a cherub, the horns of Moses, and a casket containing the breath of Christ! To a people believing implicitly in a seraph sufficiently tangible to have its proboscis preserved, the more profound issues of Judaistic philosophy must necessarily be incomprehensible. Nor is it difficult to imagine the reaction taking place in the mind of some ancient sage should he hear that a cherub--which, according to St. Augustine, signifies the Evangelists; according to Philo Judæus, the outermost circumference of the entire heavens, and according to several of the Church Fathers, the wisdom of God--had sprouted finger nails. The hopeless confusion of divine principles with the allegorical figures created to represent them to the limited faculties of the uninitiated has resulted in the most atrocious misconceptions of spiritual truths. Concepts well-nigh as preposterous as these, however, still stand as adamantine barriers to a true understanding of Old and New Testament symbolism; for, until man disentangles his reasoning powers from the web of venerated absurdities in which his mind has lain ensnared for centuries, how can Truth ever be discovered?

The Old Testament--especially the Pentateuch--contains not only the traditional account of the creation of the world and of man, but also, locked within it, the secrets of the Egyptian initiators of the *Moses* concerning the genesis of the god-man (the initiate) and the mystery of his rebirth through philosophy. While the Lawgiver of Israel is known to have compiled several works other than those generally attributed to him, the writings now commonly circulated as the purported sixth and seventh books of Moses are in reality spurious treatises on black magic foisted on the credulous during the Middle Ages. Out of the hundreds of millions of pious and thoughtful students of Holy Writ, it is almost inconceivable that but a mere handful have sensed the sublimity of the esoteric teachings of Sod (the Jewish Mysteries of Adonai). Yet familiarity with the three Qabbalistical processes termed *Gematria, Notarikon,* and *Temurah* makes possible the discovery of many of the profoundest truths of ancient Jewish superphysics.

By Gematria is meant not only the exchange of letters for their numerical equivalents but also the method of determining by an analysis of its measurements the mystic purpose for which a building or other object was constructed. S. L. MacGregor-Mathers, in *The Kabbalah Unveiled*, gives this example of the application of Gematria: "Thus also the passage, Gen. xviii. 2 *VHNH SHLSHH, Vehenna Shalisha,* 'And lo, three men,' equals in numerical value 'ALV MIKAL GBRIAL VRPAL, *Elo Mikhael Gabriel Ve-Raphael,*' These are Mikhael, Gabriel and Raphael; 'for each phrase = 701." Assuming the sides of a scalene to be 11, 9, and 6 inches, a triangle of such dimensions would then be an appropriate symbol of Jehovah, for the sum of its three sides would be 26, the numerical value of the Hebrew word IHVH. Gematria also includes the system of discovering the arcane meaning of a word by analyzing the size and arrangement of the strokes employed in the formation of its various letters. Gematria was employed by the Greeks as well as the Jews. The books of the New Testament--particularly those attributed to St. John--contain many examples of its use. Nicephorus Callistus declared the Gospel according to St. John to have been discovered in a cavern under the Temple at Jerusalem, the volume having been secreted "long anterior to the Christian æra." The existence of interpolated material in the fourth Gospel substantiates the belief that the work *was originally written without any specific reference to the man Jesus*, the statements therein accredited to Him being originally mystical discourses delivered by the personification of the Universal Mind. The remaining Johannine writings--the Epistles and the Apocalypse--are enshrouded by a similar veil of mystery.

By Notarikon each letter of a word may become the initial character of a new word. Thus from BRASHITH, first word in the book of Genesis, are extracted six words which mean that "in the beginning the Elohim saw that Israel would accept the law." Mr. MacGregor-Mathers also gives six additional examples of Notarikon formed from the above word by Solomon Meir Ben Moses, a mediæval Qabbalist. From the famous acrostic ascribed to the Erythræan Sibyl, St. Augustine derived the word ΙΧΘΥΣ, which by Notarikon was expanded into the phrase, "Jesus Christ, Son of God, Savior." By another use of Notarikon, directly the reverse of the first, the initial, last, or middle letters of the words of a sentence may be joined together to form a new word or words. For example, the name Amen, ἀμήν, maybe extracted from ארנימלרנאטז, "the Lord is the faithful King." Because they had embodied these cryptic devices in their sacred writings, the ancient priests admonished their disciples never to translate, edit, or rewrite the contents of the sacred books.

THE VISION OF EZEKIEL [9]

---

[9] From The "Bear" Bible. This plate, which is from the first Protestant Bible published in Spanish, shows the *Mercavah*, or chariot of Jehovah, which appeared to Ezekiel by the river Chebar. The prophet beheld four strange creatures (E), each having four heads, four wings, and brazen hoofs like those of a calf. And there were four wheels (F) filled with eyes. Where the

Under the general heading of *Temurah* several systems may be grouped and explained in which various letters are substituted for other letters according to prearranged tables or certain mathematical arrangements of letters, regular or irregular. Thus the alphabet may be broken into two equal parts and written in horizontal lines so that the letters of the lower row can be exchanged for those of the upper row, or vice versa. By this procedure the letters of the word *Kuzu* may be exchanged for those of IHVH, the *Tetragrammaton*. In another form of Temurah the letters are merely rearranged., שתיה is the stone which is found in the center of the world, from which point the earth spread out on all sides. When broken in two the stone is שת יה, which means "the placing of God."(See *Pekudei Rakov*, 71, 72.) Again, Temurah may consist of a simple anagram, as in the English word *live*, which reversed becomes *evil*. The various systems of Temurah are among the most complicated and profound devices of the ancient Rabbins.

---

cherubim went the wheels went also. The space between the cherubim and the wheels was filled with coals of fire. Upon the top of the chariot was a throne, upon which sat the likeness of a man (H). Ezekiel fell upon his knees when he beheld the Mercavah surrounded by a whirlwind of clouds and flames (A, B, C). A hand (K) reached out from the clouds and the prophet was ordered to eat of a scroll which the hand held forth.

According to the mystics, the wheels supporting the throne of God represent the orbits of the planets, and the entire solar system is properly the Mercavah, or chariot of God. One of the divisions of the Qabbalah--that dealing with the arts and sciences of those planes which are under the heavens--is called the Mercavah. In the Zohar it is written that the celestial throne or Ezekiel's vision signifies the traditional law; the appearance of a man sitting upon the throne represents the written law, Philo Judæus in describing the cherubim upon the Ark of the Covenant declares that the figures are an intimation of the revolutions of the whole heavens, one of the cherubim representing the outer circumference and the other the inner sphere. Facing each other, they represent the two hemispheres of the world. The flaming sword of the cherubim of Genesis is the central motion and agitation of the heavenly bodies. In all probability it also represents the solar ray.

Among theological scholars there is a growing conviction that the hitherto accepted translations of the Scriptural writings do not adequately express the spirit of the original documents.

"After the first copy of the *Book of God*," writes H. P. Blavatsky, "has been edited and launched on the world by Hilkiah, this copy disappears, and Ezra has to make a new Bible, which Judas Maccabeus finishes; * * * when it was copied from the horned letters into square letters, it was corrupted beyond recognition; * * * the Masorah completed the work of destruction; finally, we have a text, not 900 years old, abounding with omissions, interpolations, and premeditated perversions." (See *Isis Unveiled.*)

Prof. Crawford Howell Toy of Harvard notes: "Manuscripts were copied and recopied by scribes who not only sometimes made errors in letters and words, but permitted themselves to introduce new material into the text, or to combine in one manuscript, without mark of division, writings composed by different men; instances of these sorts of procedure are found especially in Micah and Jeremiah, and the groups of prophecies which go under the names of Isaiah and Zachariah." (See *Judaism and Christianity.*)

Does the mutilated condition of the Holy Bible--in part accidental--represent none the less a definite effort to confuse the uninitiated reader and thus better conceal the secrets of the Jewish *Tannaim?* Never has the Christian world been in possession of those hidden scrolls which contain the secret doctrine of Israel, and if the Qabbalists were correct in their assumption that the lost books of the Mosaic Mysteries have been woven into the fabric of the Torah, then the Scriptures are veritably books within books. In rabbinical circles the opinion is prevalent that Christendom never has understood the Old Testament and probably never will. In fact, the feeling exists--in some quarters, at least--that the Old Testament is the exclusive possession of the Jewish faith; also that Christianity, after its unrelenting persecution of the Jew, takes unwarranted liberties when it includes strictly Jewish writings in its sacred canon. But, as noted by one rabbi, if Christianity *must* use the Jewish Scriptures, it should at least strive to do so with some degree of intelligence!

In the opening chapter of Genesis it is stated that after creating light and separating it from darkness, the seven Elohim divided the waters which were under the firmament from the waters which were above the firmament. Having thus established the inferior universe in perfect accord with the esoteric teachings of the Hindu, Egyptian, and Greek Mysteries, the Elohim next turned their attention to the production of flora and fauna and lastly man. "And God said, Let us make man in *our* image, after *our* likeness. * * * So God created man in *his* own image, in the image of God created *he him*; male and female created *he them*. And God blessed them, and God said unto them, Be fruitful, and multiply, and *re*plenish the earth, * * *."

Consider in thoughtful silence the startling use of pronouns in the above extract from "the most perfect example of English literature." When the plural and androgynous Hebrew word *Elohim* was translated into the singular and sexless word *God*, the opening chapters of Genesis were rendered comparatively meaningless. It may have been feared that had the word been correctly translated as "the male and female creative agencies," the Christians would have been justly accused of worshiping a plurality of gods in the face of their repeated claims to monotheism! The plural form of the pronouns *us* and *our* reveals unmistakably, however, the pantheistic nature of Divinity. Further, the androgynous constitution of the Elohim (God) is disclosed in the next verse, where *he* (referring to God) is said to have created man in *his* own image, *male* and *female*; or, more properly, as the division of the sexes had not yet taken place, *male-female*. This is a deathblow to the time-honored concept that God is a masculine potency as portrayed by Michelangelo on the ceiling of the Sistine Chapel. The Elohim then order these androgynous beings to *be fruitful*. Note that neither the masculine nor the feminine principle as yet existed in a separate state! And, lastly, note the word "*re*plenish." The prefix *re* denotes "back to an original or former state or position," or "repetition or restoration." (See *Webster's International Dictionary*, 1926.) This definite reference to a humanity existing prior to the "creation of man" described in Genesis must be evident to the most casual reader of Scripture.

An examination of Bible dictionaries, encyclopedias, and commentaries discloses the plural form of the word *Elohim* to be beyond the comprehension of their respected authors and editors. The *New Schaff-Herzog Encyclopedia of Religious Knowledge* thus sums up the controversy over the plural form of the word Elohim: "Does it now or did it originally signify plurality of divine being?" A Dictionary of the Bible, edited by James Hastings, contains the following conclusion, which echoes the sentiments of more critical etymologists of the Bible: "The use of the plural Elohim is also difficult to explain." Dr. Havernick considers the plural form Elohim to signify the abundance and super-richness existing in the Divine Being. His statement, which appears in *The Popular and Critical Bible Encyclopædia*, is representative of the efforts made to circumvent this extremely damaging word. The *International Standard Bible Dictionary* considers the explanations offered by modern theologians--of which Dr. Havernick's is a fair example--to be too ingenious to have been conceived by the early Hebrews and maintains that the word represents the survival of a polytheistic stage of Semitic thought. *The Jewish Encyclopedia* supports the latter assumption with the following concise statement: "As far as epigraphic material, traditions, and folk-lore throw light on the question, the Semites are shown to be of polytheistic leanings."

Various schools of philosophy, both Jewish and Gentile, have offered explanations erudite and otherwise of the identity of Adam. In this primordial man the Neo-Platonists recognized the Platonic *Idea* of humanity--the archetype or pattern of the *genus homo*. Philo Judæus considered Adam to represent the human mind, which could understand (and hence give names to) the creatures about it, but could not comprehend (and hence left nameless) the mystery of its own nature. Adam was also likened to the Pythagorean *monad* which by virtue of its state of perfect unity could dwell in the Edenic sphere. When through a process akin to fission the monad became the *duad*--the proper symbol of discord and delusion--the creature thus formed was exiled from its celestial home. Thus the twofold man was driven from the Paradise belonging to the undivided creation and cherubim and a flaming sword were placed on guard at the gates of the Causal World. Consequently, only after the reestablishment of unity within himself can man regain his primal spiritual state.

According to the Isarim, the secret doctrine of Israel taught the existence of four Adams, each dwelling in one of the four Qabbalistic worlds. The first, or heavenly, Adam dwelt alone in the Atziluthic sphere and within his nature existed all spiritual and material potentialities. The second Adam resided in the sphere of Briah. Like the first Adam, this being was androgynous and the tenth division of its body (its heel, *Malchuth*) corresponded to the church of Israel that shall bruise the serpent's head. The third Adam--likewise androgynous--was clothed in a body of light and abode in the sphere of Yetzirah. The fourth Adam was merely the third Adam after the *fall* into the sphere of Assiah, at which time the spiritual man took upon himself the animal shell or *coat of skins*. The fourth Adam was still considered as a single individual, though division had taken place within his nature and two shells or physical bodies existed, in one of which was incarnated the masculine and in the other the feminine potency. (For further details consult Isaac Myer.)

The universal nature of Adam is revealed in the various accounts concerning the substances of which he was formed.

It was originally ordained that the "dirt" to be used in fashioning him was to be derived from the seven worlds. As these planes, however, refused to give of their substances, the Creator wrenched from them by force the elements to be employed in the Adamic constitution. St. Augustine discovered a Notarikon in the name of Adam. He showed that the four letters, A-D-A-M, are the first letters of the four words *Anatole Dysis Arktos Mesembria*, the Greek names for the four corners of the world. The same author also sees in Adam a prototype of Christ, for he writes: "Adam sleeps that Eve may be formed: Christ dies, that the Church may be formed. While Adam sleeps, Eve is formed from his side. When Christ is dead, His side is smitten with a spear, that there flow forth sacraments to form the church. * * * Adam himself was the figure of Him that was to come."

In his recent work, *Judaism*, George Foote Moore thus describes the proportions of the Adamic man: "He was a huge mass that filled the whole world to all the points of the compass. The dust of which his body was formed was gathered from every part of the world, or from the site of the future altar. Of greater interest is the notion that man was created androgynous, because it is probably a bit of foreign lore adapted to the first pair in Genesis. R. Samuel bar Nahman (third century), said, when God created Adam, He created him facing both ways (דיו פרעופים); then He sawed him in two and made two backs, one for each figure.

The Zohar holds the concept of two Adams: the first a divine being who, stepping forth from the highest original darkness, created the second, or earthly, Adam in His own image. The higher, or celestial, man was the Causal sphere With its divine potencies and potentialities considered as a gigantic personality; its members, according to the Gnostics, being the basic elements of existence. This Adam may have been symbolized as facing both ways to signify that with one face it looked upon the proximate Cause of itself and with the other face looked upon the vast sea of Cosmos into which it was to be immersed.

Philosophically, Adam may be regarded as representative of the full spiritual nature of man--androgynous and nor subject to decay. Of this fuller nature the mortal man has little comprehension. Just as spirit contains matter within itself and is both the source and ultimate of the state denominated *matter*, so Eve represents the lower, or mortal, portion that is taken out of, or has temporal existence in the greater and fuller *spiritual creation*. Being representative of the inferior part of the individual, Eve is the temptress who, conspiring with the serpent of mortal knowledge, caused Adam to sink into a trancelike condition in which he was unconscious of his own higher Self. When Adam seemingly awoke, he actually sank into sleep, for he no longer was in the spirit but in the body; division having taken place within him, the true Adam rested in Paradise while his lesser part incarnated in a material organism (Eve) and wandered in the darkness of mortal existence.

The followers of Mohammed apparently sensed more accurately than the uninitiated of other sects the true mystic import of Paradise, for they realized that prior to his *fall* the dwelling place of man was not in a physical garden in any particular part of the earth but rather in a higher sphere (the angelic world) watered by four mystical streams of life. After his banishment from Paradise, Adam alighted on the Island of Ceylon, and this spot is sacred to certain Hindu sects who recognize the old Island of Lanka--once presumably connected with the mainland by a bridge--as the actual site of the Garden of Eden from which the human race migrated. According to the *Arabian Nights* (Sir Richard Burton's translation), Adam's footprint may still be seen on the top of a Ceylonese mountain. In the Islamic legends, Adam was later reunited with his wife and after his death his body was brought to Jerusalem subsequent to the Flood for burial by Melchizedek. (See the *Koran*.)

The word ADM signifies a species or race and only for lack of proper understanding has Adam been considered as an individual. As the Macrocosm, Adam is the gigantic Androgyne, even the Demiurgus; as the Microcosm, he is the chief production of the Demiurgus and within the nature of the Microcosm the Demiurgus established all the qualities and powers which He Himself possessed. The Demiurgus, however, did not possess immortality and, therefore, could not bestow it upon Adam. According to legend, the Demiurgus strove to keep man from learning the incompleteness of his Maker. The Adamic man consequently partook of the qualities and characteristics of the angels who were the ministers of the Demiurgus. It was affirmed by the Gnostic Christians that the redemption of humanity was assured through the descent of Nous (Universal Mind), who was a great spiritual being superior to the Demiurgus and who, entering into the constitution of man, conferred conscious immortality upon the Demiurgic fabrications.

That phallic symbolism occupies an important place in early Jewish mysticism is indisputable. Hargrave Jennings sees in the figure of Adam a type of the lingam of Shiva, which was a stone representative of the creative power of the World Generator. "In Gregorie's works * * *," writes Jennings, "is a passage to the effect that 'Noah daily prayed in the Ark before the *Body of Adam*,' i.e., before the Phallus--Adam being the primitive Phallus, great procreator of the human race. 'It may possibly seem strange,' he says, 'that this orison should be daily said before the body of Adam,' but 'it is a most confessed tradition among the eastern men that Adam was commanded by God that his dead body should be kept above ground till a fullness of time should come to commit it פדככאלאוע to the *middle of the earth* by a priest of the Most High God.' This means Mount Moriah, the Meru of India. 'This body of Adam was embalmed and transmitted from father to son, till at last it was delivered up by Lamech into the hands of Noah.'" (See *Phallicism*.)

This interpretation somewhat clarifies the Qabbalistic assertion that in the first Adam were contained all the souls of the Israelites. (See *Sod*.) Though according to the *Aurea Legenda* Adam was buried with the three seeds of the Tree of Knowledge in his mouth, it should be borne in mind that apparently conflicting myths were often woven around a single individual. One of the profound mysteries of Qabbalism is that

64

set forth in the Notarikon based upon the letters of the name Adam (ADM). These three letters form the initials of the names *Adam, David,* and the *Messiah,* and these three personalities were said to contain one soul. As this soul represents the World Soul of humanity, Adam signifies the involving soul, the Messiah the evolving soul, and David that condition of the soul termed *epigenesis.*

In common with certain philosophic institutions of Asia, the Jewish Mysteries contained a strange doctrine concerning the *shadows of the Gods.* Gazing down into the Abyss, the Elohim beheld their own shadows and from these shadows patterned the inferior creation. "In the dramatic representation of the creation of man in the Mysteries," writes the anonymous Master of Balliol College, "the Aleim [Elohim] were represented by men who, when sculpturing the form of an Adamite being, of a man, traced the outline of it on their own shadow, or modelled it on their own shadow traced on the wall. This is how the art of drawing originated in Egypt, and the hieroglyphic figures carved on the Egyptian monuments have so little relief that they still resemble a shadow."

In the ritualism of the early Jewish Mysteries the pageantry of creation was enacted, the various actors impersonating the Creative Agencies. The *red dirt* from which the Adamic man was fashioned may signify fire, particularly since Adam is related to the *Yod,* or fire flame, which is the first letter of the sacred name *Jehovah.* In John ii. 20 it is written that the Temple was forty and six years in the building, a statement in which St. Augustine sees a secret and sacred Gematria; for, according to the Greek philosophy of numbers, the numerical value of the name *Adam* is 46. Adam thus becomes the type of the Temple, for the House of God-like primitive man--was a microcosm or epitome of the universe.

In the Mysteries, Adam is accredited with having the peculiar power of spiritual generation. Instead of reproducing his kind by the physical generative processes, he caused to issue from himself--or, more correctly, to be reflected upon substance--a shadow of himself. This shadow he then ensouled and it became a living creature. These shadows, however, remain only as long as the original figure of which they are the reflections endures, for with the removal of the original the host of likenesses vanish with it. Herein is the key to the allegorical creation of Eve out of the side of Adam; for Adam,

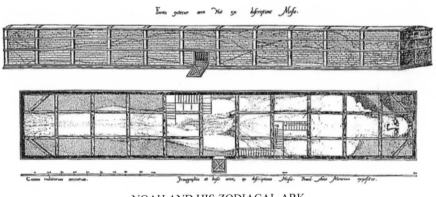

NOAH AND HIS ZODIACAL ARK
From Myer's *Qabbalah* [10]

---

[10] The early Church Father--notably Tertullian, Firmilian, St. Cyprian, St. Augustine, and St. Chrysostom--recognized in the ark a type or symbol of the Holy Catholic Church. Bede the Venerable, declared that Noah in all things typified Christ as Noah alone of his generation was just, so Christ alone was without sin. With Christ there was a sevenfold spirit of grace: with Noah seven righteous Persons. Noah by water and wood saved his own family Christ by baptism and the cross saves Christians. The ark was built of wood that did not decay. the church

representative of the *idea* or pattern, is reflected into the material universe as a multitude of ensouled images which collectively are designated *Eve*. According to another theory, the division of the sexes took place in the archetypal sphere; hence the shadows in the lower world were divided into two classes consistent with the orders established in the Archetype. In the apparently incomprehensible attraction of one sex for the other Plato recognized a cosmic urge toward reunion of the severed halves of this archetypal Being.

Exactly what is to be inferred by the division of the sexes as symbolically described in Genesis is a much-debated question. That man was primarily androgynous is quite universally conceded and it is a reasonable presumption that he will ultimately regain this bisexual state. As to the manner in

---

is composed of men who will live forever, for this ark means the church which floats upon the waves of the world.

The diagram shown above is also reproduced in *The Rosicrucians*, by Hargrave Jennings. This author adds to the original diagram appearing in Antiquitatum Judaicarum Libri IX the signs of the zodiac, placing Aries at the head and continuing in sequential order to Leo, which occupies the fifth cross section of the ark. Jennings assigns the panel containing the door to the undivided constellation of Virgo-Libra-Scorpio (which is continued into the first subdivision of the second section) and the remaining four cress sections to the constellations of Sagittarius to Pisces inclusive. A study of the plate discloses the ark to be divided into eleven main sections, and along the base and roof of each section are shown three subdivisions, thus making in all the sacred number 33. Occupying the position corresponding to the generative system of the human body will also be noted the cross upon the door of the central section. Two openings are shown in the ark: one--the main door representing the orifice through which the animal lives descend into physical existence; the other a small window proximate to the crown of the head through which the spirit gains liberty according to the ancient rites.

"When the androgenic Scorpio-Virgo was separated and the Balance or Harmony made from Scorpio, and placed between Scorpio, i.e., male, and Virgo, i.e., female, then appeared the 32 constellations or signs, as we now have them. The ark is three stories high (perhaps to symbolize Heaven, Man, Earth). In the figure of the Man, notice the parting of the hair in the middle of the forehead and the arrangement of the beard, whiskers, moustache and the hair, on the back of the neck and shoulders." (See *The Qabbalah* by Isaac Myer.)

which this will be accomplished two opinions are advanced. One school of thought affirms that the human soul was actually divided into two parts (male and female) and that man remains an unperfected creature until these parts are reunited through the emotion which man calls *love*. From this concept has grown the much-abused doctrine of "soul mates" who must quest through the ages until the complementary part of each severed soul is discovered. The modern concept of marriage is to a certain degree founded upon this ideal.

According to the other school, the so-called division of the sexes resulted from suppression of one pole of the androgynous being in order that the vital energies manifesting through it might be diverted to development of the rational faculties. From this point of view man is still actually androgynous and spiritually complete, but in the material world the feminine part of man's nature and the masculine part of woman's nature are quiescent. Through spiritual unfoldment and knowledge imparted by the Mysteries, however, the latent element in each nature is gradually brought into activity and ultimately the human being thus regains sexual equilibrium. By this theory woman is elevated from the position of being man's errant part to one of complete equality. From this point of view, marriage is regarded as a companionship in which two complete individualities manifesting opposite polarities are brought into association that each may thereby awaken the qualities latent in the other and thus assist in the attainment of individual completeness. The first theory may be said to regard marriage as an end; the second as a means to an end. The deeper schools of philosophy have leaned toward the latter as more adequately acknowledging the infinite potentialities of divine completeness in both aspects of creation.

The Christian Church is fundamentally opposed to the theory of marriage, claiming that the highest degree of spirituality is achievable only by those preserving the virginal state. This concept seemingly originated among certain sects of the early Gnostic Christians, who taught that to propagate the human species was to increase and perpetuate the power of the Demiurgus; for the lower world was looked upon as an evil fabrication created to ensnare the souls of all born into it-- hence it was a crime to assist in bringing souls to earth. When, therefore, the unfortunate father or mother shall stand before the Final Tribunal, all their offspring will also appear and accuse them of being the cause of those miseries attendant upon physical existence. This view is strengthened by the allegory of Adam and Eve, whose sin through which humanity has been brought low is universally admitted to have been concerned with the mystery of generation. Mankind, owing to Father Adam its physical existence, regards its progenitor as the primary cause of its misery; and in the judgment Day, rising up as a mighty progeny, will accuse its common paternal ancestor.

Those Gnostic sects maintaining a more rational attitude on the subject declared the very existence of the lower worlds to signify that the Supreme Creator had a definite purpose in their creation; to doubt his judgment was, therefore, a grievous error. The church, however, seemingly arrogated to itself the astonishing prerogative of correcting God in this respect, for wherever possible it continued to impose celibacy, a practice resulting in an alarming number of neurotics. In the Mysteries, celibacy is reserved for those who have reached a certain degree of spiritual unfoldment. When advocated for the mass of unenlightened humanity, however, it becomes a dangerous heresy, fatal alike to both religion and philosophy. As Christendom in its fanaticism has blamed every individual Jew for the crucifixion of Jesus, so with equal consistency it has maligned every member of the feminine sex. In vindication of Eve philosophy claims that the allegory signifies merely that man is tempted by his emotions to depart from the sure path of reason.

Many of the early Church Fathers sought to establish a direct relationship between Adam and Christ, thereby obviously discounting the extremely sinful nature of man's common ancestor, since it is quite certain that when St. Augustine likens Adam to Christ and Eve to the church he does not intend to brand the latter institution as the direct cause of the fall of man. For some inexplicable reason, however, religion has ever regarded intellectualism--in fact every form of knowledge--as fatal to man's spiritual growth. The Ignaratitine Friars are an outstanding example of this attitude.

In this ritualistic drama--possibly derived from the Egyptians--Adam, banished from the Garden of Eden, represents man philosophically exiled from the sphere of Truth. Through ignorance man falls; through wisdom he redeems himself. The Garden of Eden represents the House of the Mysteries (see *The Vision of Enoch*) in the midst of which

70

grew both the Tree of Life and the Tree of the Knowledge of Good and Evil.

Man, the banished Adam, seeks to pass from the outer court of the Sanctuary (the exterior universe) into the sanctum sanctorum, but before him rises a vast creature armed with a flashing sword that, moving slowly but continually, sweeps clear a wide circle, and through this "Ring Pass Not" the Adamic man cannot break.

The cherubim address the seeker thus: "Man, thou art dust and to dust thou shalt return. Thou wert fashioned by the Builder of Forms; thou belongest to the sphere of form, and the breath that was breathed into thy soul was the breath of form and like a flame it shall flicker out. More than thou art thou canst not be. Thou art a denizen of the outer world and it is forbidden thee to enter this inner place."

And the Adam replies: "Many times have I stood within this courtyard and begged admission to my Father's house and thou hast refused it me and sent me back to wander in darkness. True it is that I was fashioned out of the dirt and that my Maker could not confer upon me the boon of immortality. But no more shalt thou send me away; for, wandering in the darkness, I have discovered that the Almighty hath decreed my salvation because He hath sent out of the most hidden Mystery His Only Begotten who didst take upon Himself the world fashioned by the Demiurgus. Upon the elements of that world was He crucified and from Him hath poured forth the blood of my salvation. And God, entering into His creation, hath quickened it and established therein a road that leadeth to Himself. While my Maker could not give me immortality, immortality was inherent in the very dust of which I was composed, for before the world was fabricated and before the Demiurgus became the Regent of Nature the Eternal Life had impressed itself upon the face of Cosmos. This is its sign--the *Cross*. Do you now deny me entrance, I who have at last learned the mystery of myself?"

And the voice replies: "He who is aware, *IS*! Behold!"

Gazing about him, Adam finds himself in a radiant place, in the midst of which stands a tree with flashing jewels for fruit and entwined about its trunk a flaming, winged serpent crowned with a diadem of stars. It was the voice of the serpent that had spoken.

"Who art thou?" demands the Adam.

"I," the serpent answers, "am Satan who was stoned; I am the Adversary--the Lord who is against you, the one who pleads for your destruction before the Eternal Tribunal. I was your enemy upon the day that you were formed; I have led you into temptation; I have delivered you into the hands of evil; I have maligned you; I have striven ever to achieve your undoing. I am the guardian of the Tree of Knowledge and I have sworn that none whom I can lead astray shall partake of its fruits."

The Adam replies: "For uncounted ages have I been thy servant. In my ignorance I listened to thy words and they led me into paths of sorrow. Thou hast placed in my mind dreams of power, and when I struggled to realize those dreams they brought me naught but pain. Thou hast sowed in me the seeds of desire, and when I lusted after the things of the flesh agony was my only recompense. Thou hast sent me false prophets and false reasoning, and when I strove to grasp the magnitude of Truth I found thy laws were false and only dismay rewarded my strivings. I am done with thee forever, O artful Spirit! I have tired of thy world of illusions. No longer will I labor in thy vineyards of iniquity. Get thee behind me, tempter, and the host of thy temptations. There is no happiness, no peace, no good, no future in the doctrines of selfishness, hate, and passion preached by thee. All these things do I cast aside. Renounced is thy rule forever!"

And the serpent makes answer: "Behold, O Adam, the nature of thy Adversary!" The serpent disappears in a blinding sunburst of radiance and in its place stands an angel resplendent in shining, golden garments with great scarlet wings that spread from one corner of the heavens to the other. Dismayed and awestruck, the Adam falls before the divine creature.

"I am the Lord who is against thee and thus accomplishes thy salvation, " continues the voice. "Thou hast hated me, but through the ages yet to be thou shalt bless me, for I have led thee our of the sphere of the Demiurgus; I have turned thee against the illusion of worldliness; I have weaned thee of desire; I have awakened in thy soul the immortality of which I myself partake. Follow me, O Adam, for I am the Way, the Life, and the Truth!"